101 Quick-Thinking Games + Riddles for Children

SmartFun Books from Hunter House

101 Music Games for Children by Jerry Storms
101 More Music Games for Children by Jerry Storms
101 Dance Games for Children by Paul Rooyackers
101 More Dance Games for Children by Paul Rooyackers
101 Drama Games for Children by Paul Rooyackers
101 More Drama Games for Children by Paul Rooyackers
101 Movement Games for Children by Huberta Wiertsema
101 Language Games for Children by Paul Rooyackers
101 Improv Games for Children and Adults by Bob Bedore
Yoga Games for Children by Danielle Bersma and Marjoke Visscher
The Yoga Adventure for Children by Helen Purperhart
101 Life Skills Games for Children by Bernie Badegruber
101 More Life Skills Games for Children by Bernie Badegruber
101 Cool Pool Games for Children by Kim Rodomista
101 Family Vacation Games by Shando Varda
404 Deskside Activities for Energetic Kids by Barbara Davis, MS, MFA
101 Relaxation Games for Children by Allison Bartl
101 Quick-Thinking Games + Riddles for Children by Allison Bartl
101 Pep-Up Games for Children by Allison Bartl
The Yoga Zoo Adventure by Helen Purperhart

Ordering

Trade bookstores in the U.S. and Canada please contact:

Publishers Group West
1700 Fourth St., Berkeley CA 94710
Phone: (800) 788-3123   Fax: (510) 528-3444

Hunter House books are available at bulk discounts for textbook course adoptions; to qualifying community, health-care, and government organizations; and for special promotions and fund-raising. For details please contact:

Special Sales Department
Hunter House Inc., PO Box 2914, Alameda CA 94501-0914
Phone: (510) 865-5282   Fax: (510) 865-4295
E-mail: ordering@hunterhouse.com

Individuals can order our books from most bookstores, by calling **(800) 266-5592**, or from our website at
www.hunterhouse.com

101

Quick-Thinking Games + Riddles for Children

Allison Bartl

Illustrations by Klaus Puth

A Hunter House SmartFun Book

Copyright © Cornelsen Verlag Scriptor GmbH & Co. KG, Berlin 2004
Translation © 2008 Hunter House Publishers
First published in Germany in 2004 by Cornelsen as
Schnelldenker-Spiele für Grundschulkinder

Library of Congress Cataloging-in-Publication Data

Bartl, Almuth.
[Schnelldenker-spiele für Grundschulkinder. English]
101 quick-thinking games + riddles for children / Allison Bartl.
p. cm. — (SmartFun activity books)
Includes index.
Translation of: Schnelldenker-spiele für Grundschulkinder.
ISBN-13: 978-0-89793-497-8 (pbk.)
ISBN-10: 0-89793-497-0 (pbk.)
ISBN-13: 978-0-89793-498-5 (spiral bound)
ISBN-10: 0-89793-498-9 (spiral bound)
1. Games. 2. School children—Recreation. I. Title. II. Title: One hundred
and one quick-thinking games + riddles for children.
GV1203.B36413 2007
649'.55—dc22   2007034426

Project Credits

Cover Design: Jil Weil & Stefanie Gold
Illustrations: Klaus Puth
Book Production: John McKercher
Translator: Emily Banwell
Copy Editor: Kelley Blewster
Proofreader: Herman Leung
Acquisitions Editor: Jeanne Brondino
Editor: Alexandra Mummery
Publisher: Kiran S. Rana

Senior Marketing Associate: Reina Santana
Publicity Assistant: Alexi Ueltzen
Rights Coordinator: Candace Groskreutz
Order Fulfillment: Washul Lakdhon
Customer Service Manager:
 Christina Sverdrup
Administrator: Theresa Nelson
Computer Support: Peter Eichelberger

Printed and Bound by Bang Printing, Brainerd, Minnesota

Manufactured in the United States of America

9 8 7 6 5 4 3 2 1   First Edition   08 09 10 11 12

Contents

*A detailed list of the games indicating appropriate group sizes
begins on the next page.*

List of Games

List of Riddles

Introduction

There are few activities that engage people as completely as games do. When children play, they forget about the world. Once completely absorbed, they are indifferent to any kind of evaluation criteria, and to any mishaps or frustrations they may have experienced through their weaknesses. This not only alleviates existing deficits, but also increases self-confidence, which in turn is a cornerstone of successful learning.

Why Quick-Thinking Games?

These quick-thinking games and riddles encourage concentration, reasoning, patience, an understanding of numbers, the use of logic, and working with letters and words. They enhance memory skills. They help to develop social abilities and teamwork. They can be used anytime and are great for substitute teachers, free time, and enhancing math or English lessons; they provide a meaningful activity for nearly every learning situation. All the games, exercises, puzzles, and riddles included in this book can easily be modified to suit the needs of the different elementary-school grades.

Numbers are an exciting phenomenon. They encourage children to experiment, and they can be related to every aspect of life. The world becomes easier to grasp when children are able to count and calculate. The ability to calculate numbers means having power and being able to formulate things, and children quickly understand this. When they play with numbers, they increase their ability to focus calmly on a problem for a length of time and to think in a solution-oriented way. They improve their calculation skills and confidence, and many children who have problems in math class lose their shyness when playing number games, suddenly understanding the rules and having fun with them. This allows them to have successes that in turn motivate them in math class.

Logic is particularly important for the later acquisition of mathematical skills. Numbers are placed in relation to one another, calculation patterns are recognized, and ratios are determined. A number of games offered in this book help children move toward a structured way of thinking; after all, a clear overview is the first step toward a clear understanding!

As an accompaniment to the systematic approach to reading and writing taught in schools, this book offers a number of suggestions for fun and playful approaches to looking at **letters and words:** Looking for letters, writing without a writing implement, rhyming words—even if the result is sometimes just fun nonsense.

Children's achievements, as we know, are not solely dependent on their intelligence, but also on how the work is presented. Here, **concentration and patience** play an important role. Someone who is distracted easily loses track of what's going on, and may be unable to finish a task, or finishes it only with difficulty. A lack of focus is often the cause of bad grades and behavioral problems. Concentration problems are often related to a lack of interest, levels of difficulty that are too high or too low, sensory overload, emotional problems, lack of physical well-being, or poor working conditions—just to name a few. These activities provide a number of different ways to increase children's concentration through games and riddles.

Overall, the **encouragement of team spirit and social behaviors** stands in the foreground of this book. Children should be able to see their school as a place associated with positive feelings, something these activities promote.

The basis of every successful beloved children's game is fun for all participants. So go ahead and play, laugh, and be goofy with your students; do something completely unexpected for once. Laughter unites people, no matter what may be weighing on their minds. It loosens things up and is the key to every child's heart.

Key to the Icons Used in the Games

These games, riddles, and puzzles can be used with groups of children anytime, as pick-me-ups or to fill in breaks. When applicable, solutions are provided immediately after the game or riddle. The degree of difficulty increases throughout the book. Games and/or tasks for six-year-olds, for instance, can be found toward the beginning, while those for ten-year-olds are closer to the end. However, almost all the games can easily be adapted for any age. An alphabetical list of all the games and tasks can be found in the back of the book.

To help you find activities suitable for a particular situation, each one is coded with symbols or icons that tell you some things about it at a glance:

- The size of the group needed
- If props are required
- If a large space is needed
- If physical contact is or might be involved
- If the activity involves going outdoors

These are explained in more detail below.

The size of the group needed. Most of the games can be played by the whole group, but a few require pairs or small groups. (And some that are marked for the whole group can be adapted for small groups or pairs. Feel free to use your imagination.) All games are marked with one of the following icons:

 = The whole group plays together

 = The children play individually, so any size group can play

 = The children play in small groups of three or more

 = The children play in pairs

If props are required. A few activities call for the use of special items. They are flagged with the following icon:

 = Props needed

If a large space is needed. A large space is required for a few of the activities (for example, when the whole group is required to form a circle or to walk around the room). These are marked with the following icon:

 = May require a larger space

If physical contact is or might be involved. The following icon has been inserted at the activities that involve physical contact:

 = Physical contact likely

If the activity involves going outdoors. A few activities require going outdoors. These are marked with the following icon (but nearly all of the games can be played outside if lovely weather beckons):

 = Involves going outdoors

Quick Lineup

Props: Paper; pens or pencils

How to Play: The children are divided into two equal groups. The groups go to different parts of the room (or different parts of the playground if you're outside). Each child gets a slip of paper and writes down a number between one and one hundred (for younger children, use numbers between one and ten; older children can use larger numbers). Ready, set, go! The children's task is to line up in numerical order without saying a word. Children who happened to write down the same number can stand one behind the other. The group that manages this trick first wins.

2

Good Listeners

How to Play: The adult leader thinks of a specific word and makes up three sentences using that word. She reads the sentences to the group.

Examples

- Aunt Bertha will come visit **us** again soon.
- Even bad weather can't ruin this great day for **us**.
- The bus driver is going to take **us** to the museum.

The first person to figure out the word that appears in each sentence raises his hand and says the word. Try to remember it! The game continues with a new word for the next three sentences. After several rounds, who can list all the words?

"Math Chair" Race

Preparation: Move tables and chairs out of the way. Make up math problems with various solutions, at the appropriate skill level for the group.

How to Play: All the players sit together on the floor at one end of the room. The leader assigns the children numbers, but *two* children are assigned to each number. The numbers correspond to the answers of one or more of the math problems.

Children who have the same number cannot sit next to each other.

At the other end of the room is the "Math Chair," waiting for the person who can calculate the fastest. The leader then recites a math problem; for example, "100 ÷ 25." The children all do the problem; the two who have the number of the right answer, in this case four, run to the Math Chair as fast as they can. Whoever sits down first has won the round and gets a point. Then comes the next problem, maybe "12 + 5 – 9." This game requires concentration—you can't afford to stop paying attention, even for a moment. Whoever has the most points at the end of the game wins.

Variation: For advanced players, the leader can also sneak in some problems whose answer wasn't assigned to anyone. In that case, of course, nobody should be running!

What's My Job?

How to Play: A child chosen by the leader names two tools or other props that are associated with a certain job. Whoever is the first to name the right profession gets to come up with the next job riddle.

Examples

- whisk and spatula . . . . cook
- trowel and level . . . . bricklayer
- needle and scissors . . . . tailor
- hammer and saw . . . . carpenter
- brush and ladder . . . . painter
- chalk and red ink . . . . teacher
- syringe and stethoscope . . . . . doctor
- watering can and shovel . . . . . gardener
- robe and gavel . . . . judge
- red nose and giant shoes . . . . . clown

5

Word Transformation

How to Play: Everyone, including the leader, sits in a circle, facing the center. The leader starts the game by saying a short one-syllable word; for example, "dog." Then the player on her right changes one letter of the word to make a different word—"log," for instance.

The next player in line then changes a letter in this word and says "hog" or maybe "leg." The game continues until no more words can be made. The child who would have gone next then gets to come up with a new starting word.

6

Letter Switcharoo

Props: A blackboard; chalk; paper; pens or pencils

How to Play: A short word is written on the board, like "mast."

The players now have three minutes to write down as many words as possible that can be made by changing only one letter (e.g., must, mass, past, most).

The child who comes up with the most words wins the round and gets to choose the next starting word.

7

Guessing Letters

Props: An index card or small piece of paper for each letter of the alphabet; tape; a small prize

Preparation: Write the individual letters of the alphabet on separate index cards. If the group has fewer children than letters, write the extra letters on a blackboard.

How to Play: This game is fun for all elementary-age children. Each child has a letter card stuck to their back with a piece of tape. Then the children go for a stroll around the room; they ask the people they meet whether their own letter can be found in the word "car," for example, or "flower." They must only ask questions that can be answered by "yes" or "no." By process of elimination, smart questions, and deduction, each child tries to find out their own letter as quickly as possible.

Whoever thinks they have figured out the letter runs to the leader and confirms it. The three fastest letter detectives earn a small prize.

8

Just the Opposite

How to Play: One child names a word that has an opposite; for instance, "day." The first person to come up with a convincing opposite gets to choose the next word.

Examples

- day—night
- multiplication—division
- plus—minus
- captive—free
- summer—winter
- man—woman
- good—bad
- young—old
- up—down
- early—late

Athletic Letters

How to Play: The children all pair up, and when the leader calls on a pair, the two children go to the front of the room and then use their bodies to form a letter they have decided upon ahead of time.

The observers look carefully at the formation. Whoever is first to name the correct letter gets to "perform" the next letter with her partner. As a variation, several children could form a short word.

pairs

The Bean-Counting Game

Props: Twenty dried beans (or other small objects like coins, matches, etc.) for each pair of children

How to Play: The leader divides the players into pairs. In this estimating game, one player grabs a random number of beans with his right hand. He holds out his fist for his partner to see, opens it for a second, and then asks how many beans he's holding. The other player makes a guess; for instance, "There are twelve beans." Then the bean-holder opens his hand again, and they count together. The difference between the estimate and the real number is written down as minus points for the guesser.

Example: The guesser says twelve beans, and it turns out there are fourteen. The guesser receives two minus points. But then the roles are reversed, and who knows whether the other player will be a better guesser? When each player has had five turns, the scores are added up; the player with the fewest minus points wins.

Meeting

How to Play: While one child waits outside the door, the others think up a location where they'd like to "meet" her; for example, at the playground (or the zoo, the grocery store, the county fair, the airport, the circus, etc.).

The child is called back into the room and asks, "Where am I?"

Then each of the other players gets to name something one would probably see, hear, or smell at this place; for example, "I smell food cooking"; "I see waiters and waitresses"; "I hear lots of people talking." Can the child guess where she is?

Fairy-Tale Quiz

How to Play: The leader asks the group questions about well-known fairy tales. The first child who can guess the answer gets a point. At the end of the round, points are totaled.

Examples

1. Which long-haired maiden lived in a tower?
2. Who was Little Red Riding Hood going to visit when she met the wolf in the forest?
3. Which fairy-tale character lost his power once you guessed his name?
4. What were the three little pigs' houses made from?
5. What did Cinderella lose at the Prince's ball?
6. What did Snow White die of?
7. How long did Sleeping Beauty sleep?

Answers: 1. Rapunzel; 2. her grandmother; 3. Rumpelstiltskin; 4. straw, sticks, and bricks; 5. a glass slipper; 6. eating a poisoned apple; 7. one hundred years

If there's enough time, the leader can ask a much harder question; for example, "How did the frog become a prince in 'The Frog Prince'?" Most of the children will probably say it was when the princess kissed him. Then you can read them the fairy tale written by the Brothers Grimm to show that it happened when she hurled him against the wall.

Short Words

Props: Paper; pens or pencils

How to Play: Who can be the first to write down ten different three-letter nouns? Allow a set amount of time; for example, one minute. The leader or another child in the group tells everyone when their time is up.

Examples

- eat
- ice
- sea
- sun
- arm
- cow
- ant

Short Words, Long Sentences

Props: Paper; pens or pencils

How to Play: In this game, you are looking for sentences made up of only three-letter words. Each child has three minutes to come up with as long a sentence as possible. Who can make the longest one?

Examples

- The ant has hot tea.
- The bus did not let her off.
- The cow and its hat are not too hot.

15

A Different Kind
of Math Chain

How to Play: One child comes up with a math-chain problem, and the others do the problem in their heads. (Alternatively, they can use pencil and paper.) Who has the right answer?

Example: Start with the number of fingers on one hand. Add the number of wheels on a motorcycle, multiply by the number of legs on a dog, subtract the number of months in a year, and divide by the number of seasons.

Note: It's helpful if the adult leader demonstrates how to do a math chain before asking a child to try it.

What's in Common?

How to Play: One child chooses at least three other children who fit a certain criterion, and asks them to line up in front of the group. The other children guess what they have in common; for example, they're all wearing glasses, all three have blue eyes, they're all wearing sneakers.

Whoever figures out the commonality first gets to choose another characteristic and a new lineup.

pairs

All Funny Kids Plant Umbrellas

Props: Paper; a pen or marker for each pair of children

Preparation: Write the alphabet on a piece of paper in large block letters. If you will be playing this game with more than one pair of children, make as many photocopies of this paper as you think you might need.

How to Play: Two children play against each other. On the alphabet sheets they have been given, the players take turns crossing out one, two, three, or four letters in a row, starting from A. Whoever crosses out the Z wins the game.

There is a trick to winning this game every time: The person who crosses out the letters A, F, K, P, or U can be the one who gets the Z at the end. The reason is because these letters are each five letters apart counting back from Z. Since a player can only cross out four letters at a time, the one who last crosses out U can get the Z no matter what the next player does. Similarly, the one who last crosses out P can secure the U, and whoever crosses out K can secure the P, and so on. A player who knows this trick can win the game by controlling these five-letter gaps from as early as the letter A.

Example: Your partner begins and crosses out the letters A, B, and C. The next secret letter is F, so you cross out D, E, and F. Then it's your partner's turn, and so on.

Tip: In order to remember the important winning letters, just learn this sentence: **A**ll **F**unny **K**ids **P**lant **U**mbrellas. Whether or not the leader decides to share this trick with the children, and after how many rounds, is up to him.

18 Room Change

How to Play: All the children leave the room in alphabetical order according to their first names, and go into the adjoining room (or hallway, gym, playground). This must happen in complete silence. The children cannot talk, but they can communicate with signs. In the next room, they line up in the right order.

Variation: The leader gives the children a predetermined amount of time in which to complete the task. If the children succeed within that time, they are given a group reward or treat.

Race to 30

Props: Paper; pens or pencils

How to Play: The children break themselves into groups of three, and the leader helps each group decide on the order the players will follow in the game. The first player writes one to three numbers (their choice is limited to the numbers 1, 2, and 3) and adds them up (he can choose to write only 1, which is the minimum, or three 3s, which is the maximum and adds up to 9). The second player also writes anywhere from one to three numbers and adds the sum of these numbers to the first player's total. Then it's the third player's turn. The game continues until they reach thirty. Whoever has to write the number thirty loses the game.

whole
group

Proverbs

How to Play: Who can be the first to say which word in these proverbs is wrong?

- A fool and his money are soon **reunited.**
- A friend in need is a friend **agreed.**
- Look before you **sleep.**
- A bird in the **sand** is worth two in the bush.
- Variety is the spice of **cookies.**
- Don't count your **mittens** before they hatch.
- A chain is no stronger than its weakest **plank.**
- Clothes make the **plan.**
- He who laughs **fast**, laughs best.

Variation: To make this activity more competitive, the leader can write all of the proverbs on the board or on a piece of paper that is photocopied (so each child has their own copy). The children write down all of their guesses, and after a few minutes the teacher can collect their answer sheets in order to determine the winner by checking to see who had the most correct answers.

Minute Lists

How to Play: The leader divides the children into small groups of three or more players; assigns the roles of responder, timer, and counter to a child in each group; and distributes a list of the same questions to each group. Each player, in turn, is asked a question and has one minute to give as many answers as possible. Another player keeps track of the time, while someone else counts the number of appropriate answers.

Examples

- What do you need on a trip to the North Pole?
- What would you never put in your backpack?
- What can you cook in a frying pan?
- What do you take to the swimming pool with you?
- Which animals can be found in the circus?

When the minute is up, the child who was responding gets to pick out a new responder, timer, and counter for the next question.

Variation: To make this game more competitive, the groups compete against one another; the team that has the most answers to a question gets a point, and the team with the most points at the end of the game wins.

What's for Dinner?

How to Play: Ask two children to leave the room while the others decide which dish will be served today—"mashed potatoes," for example. As soon as the two children return, the whole group clearly mouths the words "mashed potatoes" over and over again, but without making a sound.

Whichever of the two players guesses the right answer first is the winner, and as a reward she gets to choose the dish for the next round. The leader then chooses two new players to leave the room while the new dish is shared with the group.

23

whole group

Letter Puzzle

Props: Paper; a marker

How to Play: One player thinks of a letter (or a word, or a number), and writes it down in block letters where the others can't see it. Then he takes a marker and traces the letter(s) in the air while describing the movements precisely to the rest of the group. Whoever is the first to guess the answer is the winner and gets the chance to write down the next letter or word.

Making Pairs

How to Play: All the children stand in pairs, with one left over. (If you have an even number of children, then the leader participates as part of a pair.) The one who is left over carefully looks at the pairs and tries to remember who is standing next to whom, and then she leaves the room. Approximately half of the pairs quickly switch partners.

Is everyone ready? The guesser is called back into the room. She tries to re-create the old order by putting the original pairs back together. The other children let themselves be moved around, even if the guesser is wrong. Once the guesser is finished, any mistakes are pointed out, and a good memory is rewarded with a round of applause.

Who wants to try next?

Different Uses

How to Play: One child names an object; for instance, "newspaper." The others try to think up other uses for the object. The more original and unusual the ideas, the better. A newspaper could be used as a rug or as a flyswatter. It could be recycled as toilet paper or as lining for a birdcage. It could be a warm blanket, or crumpled up and used as a ball.

The leader can take notes on the board or count the ideas. After three or more rounds, see which object inspired the most ideas. Whoever came up with that object is the winner.

26

whole group

Clapping Songs

How to Play: One child thinks of a simple song that everyone knows, like "Jingle Bells," and claps out the rhythm. Who can recognize the song first and say its name? The winner of the first round gets to clap out the next song.

whole group

A Place to Stand

Prop: Chalk

Preparation: On the playground or some other paved surface, use chalk to draw an eight-by-eight grid. Each square should be big enough for a child to stand in.

How to Play: At the beginning of the game, each child stands in one of the squares. At the leader's signal, each child moves to a new square bordering the first one, either diagonally, horizontally, or vertically. As they move, the leader crosses out one of the squares at random. That square is now off limits. The game continues until there are fewer and fewer open squares left, and more and more children are out when they run out of places to move. The winner is the one who chooses her position strategically and keeps finding a spot to stand in until the very end.

Rhyming Journeys

How to Play: The players sit in a circle, facing the center. The leader chooses a player to start, and he does so by saying where he's going. Then, the player on his left has to come up with a rhyme for what he will do there. It might go like this: "I'm traveling to Timbuktu...," and the next player continues, "...and eating peanuts in the zoo."

The next child on the left might then add, "...and putting polish on my shoe."

Or: "I'm on my way to San Jose...," "...and while I'm there I'll see a play."

Or: "My destination is New York...," "...where I'll eat some cheesecake with a fork."

The children take turns one after the other, following their order in the circle. If a player can't think of a rhyme, they have to name the next destination.

The Number-Croaking Frog

How to Play: One child begins by saying, "I know a frog who always croaks like this: 2, 4, 6, 8...." The others listen carefully to the series of numbers, and quickly decide how it continues. Whoever is the first to come up with the next number, in this case "10," gets to croak the next four-number series.

Examples
- 10, 20, 30, 40...
- 2, 4, 8, 16...
- 1, 4, 9, 16...

any
size

How Many Stars in the Sky?

Props: Paper; pens or pencils

Preparation: Prepare a list of trivia questions (see examples below)

How to Play: Nobody can really answer that question, but there are a few others that they probably can. On a piece of paper, each child answers a series of questions the leader has prepared. If they don't know the answer, they make a guess. Whoever has the most correct answers wins.

Examples

- How many dwarfs lived with Snow White?
- How many days are there in the month of December?
- How many grades are there at your school?
- How many pints of soup can be served from a two-gallon pot?
- How many pins are there in a bowling game?
- How many Olympic rings are there?

- How many days are there in a week?
- How many hours are there in a day?
- How many letters are there in the alphabet?
- How many dots are there on a die?
- How many players are there on a baseball team?
- How many days are there in a leap year?
- How many letters are in the word "committee"?
- How many seasons are there?

Playing-Card Concentration

Props: A deck of playing cards

How to Play: Between three and five children can play this concentration game at once. Twenty playing cards are arranged face up in four rows. The leader of the game names one of the cards; for instance, "King of Hearts." The children use just their eyes to look for the card (in other words, they don't point or gesture). Whoever is the first to find the card located to the right of the King of Hearts and calls its value out loud ("Queen," for example) gets a point. If the King of Hearts is on the right end of a row, then the card to be called out is the one at the beginning of the row. The leader can also determine that the card to be called out should be to the left, above, or below, etc. To make the game more exciting, the leader can give a different direction each time (for example, "Five of Spades; above," and then "Ace of Diamonds; left"). Whoever has the most points after about ten rounds shuffles the cards thoroughly, lays them back out in four rows, and takes over as the game leader.

32

Similarities

How to Play: A child names two things; for example, "ice cube and snow-man." The others must guess what the two have in common. In this case, both are cold. Whoever is the first to discover the similarity poses the next riddle.

Examples

- Sheep and snail: both are animals, or both begin with "s."
- Peanut and orange: both are foods, or both have an outside you can't eat.

whole group

Nonsense

How to Play: Who can think of the funniest answer to these questions?

1. What hops from one lily pad to the next and says, "Moo"?
2. What wears green and swings from branch to branch in the forest?
3. What's yellow, juicy, and goes up and down?
4. How can you keep a camel from going through the eye of a needle?

Possible answers: 1. A frog with a speech impediment; 2. A monkey in a dragon costume; 3. A lemon in an elevator; 4. Tie a knot in his tail.

Can you think of any other funny questions?

34

Tommy Traps
the Texan Trout

How to Play: Divide the group into pairs. Each child thinks of a sentence in which every word begins with the same letter. Whoever makes up the longest sentence wins. The children choose which letters they want to play with.

Example: This Tuesday, Tommy trapped the Texan trout to test Timmy's traps.

whole group

35

Lowest Number

Props: A blackboard, overhead projector, or big piece of paper; a writing utensil

How to Play: Before starting, the leader assigns an order to the players (i.e., by following seat assignments, by having the children line up, or by random). The leader then writes a random assortment of numbers on the board (or an overhead projector, or a big piece of paper). There should be one number for each player. The first player picks out the lowest number from this disorderly group, and says it out loud. The next person names the second lowest number, and so on until the last player finally reads the highest number.

This concentration game is easier if someone follows along and circles or crosses out the numbers as they are called out.

Note: To make this game more competitive, players who take more than one second to say their number or who say the wrong number are "out." The last player(s) remaining is then rewarded with a small treat or prize.

Voice Memory

How to Play: One child stands with her back to the rest of the group. Whichever player chooses to start says "pumpernickel" loudly and clearly; then another says it, then a third; then maybe the first person says it again. There should be at least four "pumpernickels" before the guesser turns around. She then tries to guess which children spoke, and in which order.

If she guesses incorrectly, she gets to choose a new person to be the guesser. If she guesses correctly, she gets to go again, but each time she gets things right, one more "pumpernickel" should be added to the next round to make things more difficult. Who is the best at guessing correctly?

Where's the Candy?

Props: Eight empty matchboxes; some pieces of candy

How to Play: The leader places eight identical empty matchboxes on the table. As the children watch, the leader places a piece of candy in one of the boxes. Then the boxes are shuffled around on the table. The children must watch carefully and follow the candy box with their eyes. Finally, they are asked, "Where's the candy?" Each child makes a guess, and whoever guesses correctly gets a piece of candy as a reward.

The Surprise Box

Props: A box, basket, shopping bag, or backpack

How to Play: The adult leader thinks up a category for all the contents of the box, and the children must guess the category. The leader looks into the box (or basket, shopping bag, backpack, etc.) and says, for example, "The surprise box has an apple, a cherry, and a strawberry in it." Whoever is the first to call out "fruit" in this case is on the right track; the person who guesses "red fruit" has the correct answer and wins.

Then it's time to look in the box again. This time there's a parka, thermal underwear, a sweater, two pairs of wool socks, and a hat. "Winter clothing" is the right answer for this one. But then it gets harder: Mrs. Fisher, Karla, Mr. Holman, and Jenny are spotted in the surprise box. This should be no problem for smart kids, who remember that all those people wear glasses.

whole group

One-Legged Letters

How to Play: A child hops on one leg, spelling out the shape of a letter or number. The others watch carefully. Whoever is first to name the correct letter gets to take the next turn and "hop" a letter.

Variation: In the winter, you might be able to make the letters (or numbers) in the snow.

whole
group

Quick Neighbors

How to Play: All the players sit in a circle and close their eyes. The teacher calls out the name of one of the children—"Tim," for example. Tim doesn't move a muscle when he hears his name, but the people sitting on either side of him have to react quickly. Whichever of the two is first to call out "Here!" wins a point for paying attention. Of course, their eyes stay closed the whole time. At the end of the game, attention points can be traded in for gummy bears, nuts, or similar prizes.

Counting Letters

How to Play: Divide the children into small groups. One of the children chooses and says aloud a random word and a number; for instance, "January, five." The others picture the word in their heads, count the letters, and call out the letter that matches the number. For this example, it would be "a," because the fifth letter in the word is "a." Whoever solves it first gets to make up the next puzzle.

Famous People

How to Play: Divide the children into small groups. One child thinks of a famous person or character whom everyone knows, and tells about his or her life. The others listen carefully and try to guess who it is. Whoever is first to guess correctly gets to choose the next mystery person. Whoever guesses wrong is out until the end of the game.

Examples
- Santa Claus
- the Easter Bunny
- Mickey Mouse
- Spongebob Squarepants
- Little Red Riding Hood
- Harry Potter

whole group

Stand Up!

Props: Big pieces of paper with different numbers written on them, as explained below

Preparation: Draw different numbers on big pieces of paper. There should be one piece of paper for each child.

How to Play: Each child holds a big piece of paper with a different number written on it and sits in a chair. They make sure to remember the number they are holding. One child is in charge of leading the game, and she names specific groups of numbers; for example, if she says, "All the even numbers!" all the children with even numbers stand up and hold their numbers high. The game leader checks the numbers (and also whether anyone has forgotten to stand up) and then gives the signal to sit down.

Then the leader might call out, "All numbers smaller than fifteen!"
Or: "All numbers bigger than twenty but smaller than thirty!"
The faster the game is played, the more exciting it is.

44

Stand-Up Words

Props: Big pieces of paper with different letters written on them, as explained below

Preparation: Draw different letters of the alphabet on big pieces of paper. There should be one piece of paper for each child.

How to Play: Each child holds a big piece of paper with a letter written on it. The leader names words made up of all different letters; for example, "storm." Everyone whose letter is part of the word stands up. The children can line up next to each other to check whether the word is right.

Tip: When assigning letters, pay attention to which ones will actually be used. Avoid less common letters like X or Q.

Variation: To make this game more competitive, the leader should give the children a set time limit of five to ten seconds to form the word. If a child forgets to line up or stands in the wrong order, they are eliminated and give their letter to the remaining player of their choosing. Whoever is still in when the leader decides to end the game wins and is given a small reward.

Double Trouble

How to Play: The players are divided into two groups. They're looking for words that consist of two identical syllables, such as papa, pom-pom, yo-yo, mama, dodo. As soon as a child comes up with a good example, her group receives a point. The game is played until one group manages to pull ahead of the other group by three points.

Good Neighbors

How to Play: This game can be played in small groups. One child names a letter at random; for example, "T," and calls on another child who then has a few seconds to name the letter's neighbors, in this case "S" and "U." If the answer is correct, the second child comes up with another letter and calls on a different child to name the neighboring letters. If the answer is incorrect or partially incorrect, the player simply starts over with a new letter.

Variation: To make this game more competitive, turn it into an elimination game in which players who guess correctly are "out" and whoever remains when the leader ends the game are the winners.

47

Ping-Pong Words

How to Play: This game can be played in small groups. One player says any sentence, but leaves out an important word and replaces it with as many "pings" and "pongs" as there are syllables in the word. For instance, the player might say, "For my birthday I want a new ping-pong-ping." Now the listeners know the word is a three-syllable noun. Whoever comes up with an answer that works wins. The solution does not have to be the word that the first player had in mind. He might have wished for a new "bicycle," but another player calls out "PlayStation." This solution is fine, too, because it fits with the sentence and has the right number of syllables.

Which word fits into this sentence? "Tomorrow evening the ping-pong-ping is coming." (E.g., tooth fairy, elephant, microwave, hurricane....)

Transcription

Props: A blackboard or overhead projector; a marker or chalk for writing

How to Play: Pick one child to be the writer, who will stand at the black-board (or overhead projector), and another child to stand behind her. The second child thinks of a word he wants to spell out and begins tracing it on the first child's back, one letter at a time. As the writer figures out which letter is being traced on her back, she writes it on the board. The rest of the group watches carefully to see if they can guess the mystery word. Whoever is the first to figure it out gets to write the next word on the blackboard and choose a new back tracer.

49

Fuzzlewug

How to Play: One player leaves the room, and the others come up with an object they will call "fuzzlewug" from now on. For example, the word to be replaced might be the word "hat." The player is called back into the room. He calls on three children to give him true sentences where the secret word is replaced by "fuzzlewug," such as, "I only wear my fuzzlewug in the winter."

Or: "Last winter I lost two fuzzlewugs."

Or: "My grandma knits me a new fuzzlewug every year."

Can the guesser figure out the secret word behind "fuzzlewug"? If not, he may ask to hear some more sentences.

Variation: To make this game more competitive, if a player guesses the word correctly after only hearing the three sentences, she gets to choose the next word to be replaced as well as the next guesser. Players who don't guess the proper word are still allowed to play, but the leader gets to choose the next guesser and the next word being replaced.

pairs

Headless Mother

Props: Paper; pens or pencils

How to Play: Divide the group into pairs. Each team chooses a scribe who has to write down all the words the team can come up with that can lose their first letter and still make sense. Who can think of the most examples within five minutes?

Examples

- mother—other
- bread—read
- feat—eat
- dear—ear
- bring—ring

Mystery Object

How to Play: The children divide into two equal groups and sit in different parts of the room. Each group secretly decides on an object; for example, a lightbulb, bottle cap, or glasses case and then pick a representative to send to the other team. The children in each group ask the representative as many questions about the other team's object as they want, as long as they can be answered truthfully with a "yes" or "no."

Which team will guess the other team's object first and score the winning point?

Walking Around
the Square

Props: Paper; pens or pencils

How to Play: Each player draws a grid with sixteen boxes, four by four. Horizontally, the boxes are labeled A, B, C, and D; vertically, they are labeled from 1 to 4. A little man is drawn in the top left corner (A1). The player's task is to find a way for the little man to walk through all the squares on the grid without crossing the same square twice. The little man must end up back in the starting square at the end.

Whoever is the first to find the solution is the winner, of course!

Possible solution: A1, B1, C1, D1, D2, C2, B2, B3, C3, D3, D4, C4, B4, A4, A3, A2, A1 (see illustration)

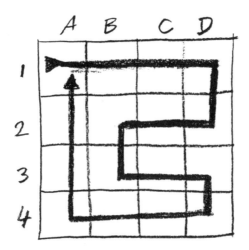

whole group

Damp Letters

Props: A blackboard (or outdoor pavement); a damp sponge

How to Play: With a damp sponge, write two letters on the board; for instance, "r" and "e." The players must come up with words that begin with "r" and end with "e." They have as much time as it takes for the damp letters to disappear. Whoever comes up with the most words wins and gets to choose the next two letters.

Possible solutions: rattle, rite, rope, rhyme, role...

Variation: This game can be played outside. Use a damp sponge to write on the concrete pavement.

Locked In

How to Play: The adult leader lists three words, each of which has another word hidden in it. The players try to figure out the hidden word. Whoever calls out the correct answer first wins.

Examples

- handle, wander, landed (and)
- metal, comet, plummet (met)
- shout, mouth, about (out)
- alone, scone, phone (one)
- bone, honest, contract (on)
- plate, breathe, matter (at)

Some words even have *two* words in them:

- twisty, stylish, misty (is, sty)

At Your Fingertips

Props: Ten different objects; a blindfold; a table

How to Play: A treasure trove of ten different objects is spread out on the table (or outside on a blanket on the lawn). The objects could include a key, a hair clip, a ring, a chalkboard eraser, etc. Pick one child to be the "blind person" and one to be a "thief." Lead the blind person to the table, where he has exactly thirty seconds to memorize the objects before he is blindfolded. Then the thief sneaks up, steals one of the objects, and moves the other ones around. Once this has been done, the "blind person" starts to feel the remaining objects. He should try to determine as quickly as possible which object has gone missing.

Variation: The game is especially exciting if you also give the thief a small assignment: rolling three sixes with a set of dice, for example, or hopping across the room (or around the blanket) on one leg. The "blind person" wins if she can guess the missing object before the thief has finished his assignment. If not, the thief wins the game. Whoever wins gets to pick the next two children to play.

whole group

Name Jumble

Props: Paper; pens or pencils

How to Play: Each child arranges the letters in her name in alphabetical order, and writes down the alphabetized name on a slip of paper. The pieces of paper are collected and given to one player. He draws a slip of paper, unfolds it, and reads the name out loud—for instance, "ACEHILM."

Everyone ponders what the name could be. (The alphabetized name could be written on the board to make this easier.) Whoever figures out the answer first and calls out "Michael" (in this case) is the winner, and gets to draw the next name.

Meaningful Names

How to Play: Can you make up a more or less meaningful sentence using the letters of your first name as initials?

Lisa might come up with a sentence like "Let's invite some alligators." Mark could make one like this: "Many animals read Kipling." Naturally, you could then move on to making sentences for last names, for all the teachers' names, for brothers and sisters, aunts and uncles, dogs and cats....

58

Single-Syllable Auction

How to Play: We're looking for one-syllable words with as many letters as possible. One child plays the role of the auctioneer. She asks for the first bid. Whoever thinks of a single-syllable word first, such as "dog," places it as a minimum bid. The next child to come up with a longer single-syllable word, such as "duck," then outbids him. The next child to think of a longer word, such as "truck," then places her bid. Since this word has five letters, it stands as the high bid unless someone else comes up with a longer one-syllable word, like "freeze."

Finally, the auctioneer calls out, "Going once, going twice, sold!" and bangs her fist on the table. Whoever came up with the last word is the winner, and then the bidding starts again.

small groups

Multiplication Race

Props: Cards with numbers written on them, as explained below

Preparation: Choose a number, such as 4. On five cards, write down various multiples of 4, one on each card (e.g., 12, 20, 24, 36, 40). Make several sets of cards, using a different multiplier for each set.

How to Play: Divide the group into teams of five. Select one team to go first. Each child on the team is given a card, each of which has written on it the multiple of a certain number, such as 4 (see example above). The team's main task is to figure out which number is being multiplied in their set of cards. Once they've done that, they line up in numerical order as quickly as possible. The first team to line up properly wins.

Example: The children on one team receive the following cards: 12, 36, 20, 24, 40. (Tip: In this case, the adult leader should probably tell the children that they're looking for an answer *other than* 2.) Once they've figured out that the common multiplier is 4, they line up in this order: 12, 20, 24, 36, 40. Another child keeps track of the time.

After that, another group can try to beat the record using a different set of numbers, or two teams can play simultaneously. In that case, the first team to line up in the right order is the winner.

60

Dreamland

How to Play: Divide the group into small teams. One player thinks up a characteristic that applies to all the things in his "dreamland." For example, all the names of people, animals, plants, and objects might contain a double consonant. Then the player cheerfully begins to describe his dreamland to the other players: "In my dreamland there are giraffes, but no elephants. There are butterflies, but no wasps; poppies, but no roses; carrots, but no beans; cottages, but no cabins; dinners, but no lunches," etc.

Whoever is the first to come up with the dreamland's unusual requirement is the winner and gets to think up and describe to the group the criteria for her dreamland.

Other possible characteristics

- All the objects have one or two of the same vowels.
- Everything makes a sound.
- Everything is very small, or is the same color.

Math Bingo

Props: A sheet of paper with a blank four-by-four grid on it for each child; pens or pencils

How to Play: Hand out the grids. Now slowly give the group sixteen math problems, one after the other. The children write down the answers in any order they like, filling in all the squares. This will create many different grids, all with (hopefully) the same numbers on them, but in different locations.

Then the leader calls out the numbers in random order, and the players cross out the numbers as they are called. The first person to cross out four consecutive squares horizontally, vertically, or diagonally calls out "Bingo!" and is the winner.

Dice Roll-Off

Props: Several pairs of dice; paper; pens or pencils

How to Play: The leader divides the group into an even number of small teams, and pairs up the teams so each team has an opposing team to face off against. Each team receives a pair of dice, and before the game starts, each child rolls one die to determine the order players will follow in the game. To start the game, two teams face off against each other. One child from each group is up at a time. He or she rolls two dice, multiplies the numbers (for example, 6 × 3 = 18), and writes down the number of points. Then the next player is up. Move quickly and pay attention! The game continues until one team reaches 100 points and is declared the winner. All the children in the group should count along in their heads so they will know when they've gotten to 100.

Forward and Backward

Props: Identical copies of a fairy tale or a familiar text for each child

How to Play: All the children have copies of a familiar text (a fairy tale, for example) in front of them. One child begins to read out loud. The reader may stop at any point and call on another child. The second child—providing she was paying close attention—now begins at the same spot and reads the text backward, word for word. She, too, can stop at any point and call on another child, who will continue reading in the right direction. This forward-and-backward reading continues until the leader gives the sign to stop.

Variation: To make this activity more competitive, it can be turned into an elimination game in which players who lose their place are "out," and players who are still "in" when the leader ends the game are winners who are given a reward or treat for having good concentration.

Words in a Square

Props: Letter cards or tiles. If you have a Scrabble game, use those tiles; otherwise, use index cards or small pieces of paper. Write down each vowel once and each consonant three times (one letter per card). Each child also needs paper and pen or pencil.

How to Play: Each player draws a five-by-five grid of equal-sized squares on a piece of paper. Meanwhile, the letter tiles or index cards are shuffled well and placed in a small bag. Once all the players are finished drawing their grids, the leader draws a letter from the bag and reads it aloud; for example, "K." Each player finds a spot for the K on her or his grid, and writes it there. Once everyone is ready, the leader draws the next letter, and so on, until all twenty-five squares have been filled. As they write their letters, the players must position them so that their grids contain as many words as possible, and that they are as long as possible. The words can run horizontally, vertically, or diagonally. Players cannot change the position of any letters they've already written on their grid.

   Scoring: Words with two letters are worth one point. Words with three letters receive three points. Words with four letters are worth five points. If someone manages to make a five-letter word, he or she is awarded ten points. The person with the most points at the end wins.

whole group

The Alphabet-Shift Code

Props: A blackboard; chalk

How to Play: A strange word is written on the board; for example, NPOEBZ. Players try to figure out the real word by substituting each letter with the one immediately preceding it in the alphabet: Monday.

In the following word, you can substitute the letters with the *succeeding* letters in the alphabet: VHMSDQ (winter).

The leader writes a list of these strange words on the board. The first person to figure out all the words raises her hand and reads the answers. If she is correct, she wins and a new word is chosen by the leader.

Variation: The leader writes an entire sentence on the board; for instance, "All the teachers are wearing funny hats today."

Then the children count off (1, 2, 1, 2, 1, 2...) to form two groups. Group 1 "translates" the sentence into preceding letters, and Group 2 into succeeding letters.

After ten minutes, the leader calls out, "Stop!" Each child counts how many words have been "translated" into the letters just before or after the original.

Each completed word receives a point. Which group will win?

The Bell-and-Whistle Multiplication Table

Props: A number of bells, squeaky toys, or other noisemakers

How to Play: The leader places the noisemakers on the floor and has the children sit in a circle around them. He picks one child to start as well as the direction in which the game will go around the circle. The multiples of certain numbers are replaced by noises. For example, using multiples of three, the first child begins to count, saying, "One." The next says, "Two." Whoever is next, having reached a multiple of three, reaches for a bell and rings that instead. Whenever a multiple of three is reached, that same bell is rung. The order goes: "One, two, [jingle], four, five, [jingle]," etc.

In the next round, in addition to the bell, a squeaky toy is used to replace all multiples of four, so now the group is using noisemakers for multiples of both three and four. The counting continues: "One, two, [jingle], [squeak], five, [jingle], seven, [squeak]...."

In the third round, a tambourine might be added to replace the multiples of five; then a key ring or some other noisemaker might join in the game for multiples of six.

Look out—if a number (like twelve) is divisible by more than one other number, all the replacement noises come into play!

The Extraterrestrial Multiplication Table

How to Play: On the planet Mars, the strangest Martians have been spotted. These creatures have the most unusual traits: If one of them laughs too hard, he pops and goes "SPLAT."

This game works well when players sit in a circle, as the order the players must follow is then easy to see. To start the game, the leader picks one child to lead off as well as the direction in which the game will go. This child lists the creature's traits: "One Martian has four legs, three eyes, two antennae, and nine green hairs. If he laughs too hard, he goes 'SPLAT.' " The second child continues, "Two Martians have eight legs, six eyes, four antennae, and eighteen green hairs; and if they laugh too hard, they go 'SPLAT SPLAT.' "

The game goes on until ten Martians have been described. Then the whole thing is repeated in reverse: "Nine Martians have thirty-six legs, twenty-seven eyes...."

Whoever makes a mistake is out, and the next player starts where the previous player left off. Who will be the last one left?

Alphabetical Categories

Props: A piece of paper for each player; pens or pencils

How to Play: Each player writes the letters of the alphabet down the left side of a piece of paper.

Give the children a large category; for example, "Jobs." The players have exactly five minutes to write down appropriate examples, one for each letter of the alphabet: auto mechanic, baker, chemist, doorman, electrician, etc. Once the time is up, the children trade sheets and score them. Each appropriate word is given one point. The winner is whoever receives the most points.

Some possible general categories:

- colors (apple green, blue, copper, dark orange...)
- things you can find in an aquarium
- zoo animals
- food
- Spanish words
- pets' names

Beep!

How to Play: Divide the children into pairs. Each pair decides on a word, starting with a shorter one like "beg" and in later turns working up to longer words like "expectation," "meteorology," or "abracadabra." The players take turns reciting the alphabet one letter at a time; however, all the letters found in their word are left out and replaced with "beep." For "beg," for example, they would say, "A," "Beep," "C," "D," "Beep," "F," etc. What makes this game challenging is that the partners take turns saying one letter at a time, inserting "beep" as applicable.

Each player needs to pay close attention to make sure the other one doesn't make any mistakes. This game is both extremely helpful for spelling and an excellent concentration game.

Variation: To make this game more competitive, turn it into an elimination game as follows: If a player makes a mistake they are out, but in the next round their partner gets to challenge another player who is still in. Whoever remains at the end of the game is the overall winner.

Alphabet Substitute

Props: Reading material (e.g., a short newspaper article, a recipe, instructions for operating a vacuum cleaner)

How to Play: Divide the class into small groups. Give each group a copy of the chosen reading material. Based on an order predetermined by the leader (e.g., based on seat assignment), each player takes a turn reading a few sentences aloud, but as they read they replace all the Rs with Bs (or maybe all the Ts with Ps, etc.). This isn't easy, and it's so funny to listen to that you end up laughing more than reading.

The other players listen carefully—each R (or T, etc.) that the reader lets slip is punished with a minus point. Who gets the best score?

Word Pyramid

Props: A blackboard; chalk

How to Play: The leader writes a two-letter word at the top of the black-board; for example, "IT." The children add some other letter to it in order to create another word; for instance, "TIP." (The letters can be rearranged to create the new word.) The leader writes the new word directly beneath the first word. Then a fourth letter is added—an S, maybe, to create the word "PITS." The object is to build as tall a pyramid as possible. When the pyramid can't be made any bigger, the last player who was able to add a letter is considered the winner of that round and gets to choose a new two-letter word.

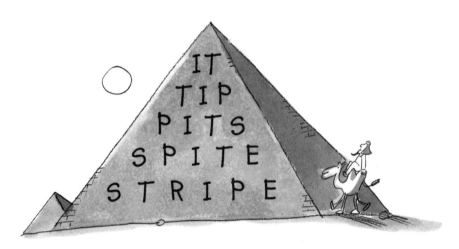

Variation: The game can also be played verbally, without the visual aid of the pyramid. Then it becomes a game of concentration as well.

small groups

Verb Dice

Prop: A die for each group

How to Play: For this fast-paced game, eight or so children sit around a table. The leader picks one child in each group to start, and tells the players the direction they will go in the circle. The leader also picks one player to be the judge. The judge announces the letter that all verbs must start with, counts the responses, and makes sure no verbs are repeated. The players then take turns rolling a die until someone rolls a six. This child now names as many verbs as possible that start with C: crawl, climb, clap, chuckle, croon, etc.

climb
crawl
clap
chuckle
croon
cross

Meanwhile, the other children keep rolling the die. As soon as someone else rolls a six, the first child's turn is over, and the new roller gets to start listing verbs that start with a different letter—B, for instance.

A judge watches to make sure no words are repeated; she or he keeps track of the results and provides the initial letters. Naturally, you can play this with different types of words (nouns, adjectives, etc.).

Variation: To make this game more competitive, the player (or players) who comes up with the most valid responses—regardless of the letter—is the winner.

73

In-Between Words

Props: Paper; pens or pencils

How to Play: The players have three minutes to write down as many words as possible that could come between "rabbit" and "runny (nose)" in the dictionary. Then the children's answers are read aloud. Whoever has come up with the most words is the winner.

Examples

- rainbow
- rake
- ramp
- read
- roof
- rug

Tip: If the game is being played with a large group, the words can be written on the board. The first person to put all the words in alphabetical order is the winner, and gets a big round of applause!

Sports Quiz

Props: Paper; pens or pencils

How to Play: Each child writes down as many kinds of sports as possible that require a ball. After two minutes of writing time, the answers are read aloud. Whoever came up with the most is the winner.

Examples

- tennis
- ping-pong
- golf
- soccer
- handball
- volleyball
- basketball

Sports Homonyms

How to Play: Tell the children that a word with more than one meaning is a homonym. Then see if they can come up with the answers to the following questions. In the case of these homonyms, one of the meanings of each word has to be related to sports or be a part of a sport's terminology.

1. What's something you need for all kinds of different games and is also the name for a big fancy dance party?
2. What is a piece of jewelry and is also the place where you would find two boxers during a match?
3. What is a beautiful, delicate insect and also a swim stroke?

Answers: 1. ball; 2. ring; 3. butterfly

Counting or Measuring?

Props: Paper; pens or pencils

How to Play: The leader names various things that can either be counted or measured. The children write down "c" if the object can be counted or "m" if it can be measured.

Examples
- a walk around the block (m)
- children on the playground (c)
- a fever (m)

- weight (m)
- buttons on a coat (c)
- pens in your backpack (c)
- water (m)

This can be made into a contest by seeing who had the most correct answers, or the children can simply read the letters in order—in this case, m, c, m, m, c, c, m.

Variation for older children: They either write down "piece" for everything that can be counted, or the correct measuring unit for the measurable things. For the example above, the answers would be: feet (yards, miles), piece, degrees, pounds, piece, piece, ounces (quarts, gallons, etc.).

any size

Remainder Lotto

How to Play: For this game, decide on a two-digit number; for instance, 12. Then multiply the number by ten, in this case, 120. Say both numbers out loud to the group. Then chose a player to start, who must then call out a number between 12 and 120, let's say 46.

The other children figure out how many times 12 goes into this number (46 ÷ 12 = 3 r10), and then write down only the remainder (10).

Then the player who started the game calls out nine more numbers between 12 and 120. Allow players time to do the division in between. The remainders are read aloud and compared; the winners are the ones who wrote down the most correct answers.

Example: The player names the following numbers: "46, 112, 79, 29, 96, 18, 31, 64, 75, 50," and the others write down the remainders: "10, 4, 7, 5, 0, 6, 7, 4, 3, 2."

78

Alphabetical Words

Props: Paper; pens or pencils

How to Play: The children have exactly five minutes to list as many words as possible whose letters appear in alphabetical order; for example, egg, lot, fin, ant, cell, etc.

Whoever comes up with the most words is the winner.

Same Beginning, Same Ending

Props: Paper; pens or pencils

How to Play: We're looking for as many words as possible that begin and end with the same letter. The leader calls out a letter, and all the children start writing. After two minutes, the answers are read aloud. Whoever has listed the most words is the winner and gets to choose the next letter.

Examples
- d: deed, dead, dad, dud
- t: trot, treat, tart, tent
- r: rear, reader, roar, ranger
- c: cryptic, cleric, cosmic, comic

Word Race

Props: Paper; pens or pencils

How to Play: The children sit with paper and pencils ready. The leader announces two letters; for example, "u-l" (o-n, i-n, i-l, etc.). The object is to list as many four-letter words as possible that contain these two letters in the middle. For "u-l": bull, mule, gulp, full, pulp, bulb, rule, etc. Whoever comes up with the most words within three minutes wins.

whole group

Pass the Story

Props: Objects such as nuts, coins, etc.

How to Play: The children all sit in a circle on the floor. In the middle of the circle are some nuts (or coins, oranges, etc.)—one fewer than the number of children playing. One child begins reading a story. At some point he stops unexpectedly and grabs one of the nuts. The listeners all try to get one for themselves, too. One listener will go empty-handed, and that means she should pick up the book and continue reading. The listeners put their nuts back in the middle, and the game starts over.

whole
group

What's Next?

How to Play: Who can guess what number comes next in each series?

- 50, 45, 40, 35…?
- 1, 2, 4, 8, 16…?
- 11, 22, 33, 44…?
- 10, 19, 37, 73, 145…?

The child who guesses correctly first is given a small treat or reward.

Solution: 30 (–5); 32 (×2); 55 (+11); 289 (×2–1)

Variation: The children are given one minute to review the four series and write down their guesses. When time runs out, the leader checks everyone's guesses and gives a prize to the child or children who got the most answers correct.

83

Estimation

Props: Paper; pens or pencils

How to Play: In order to distract the group, or to keep them occupied quietly for a few minutes, try the following question: "How long do you think it would take to count from one to one billion, assuming you said one number every second?" (Hint: The answer we're looking for is not "one billion seconds.")

After a few minutes of calculating, each person writes their answer on a slip of paper and trades with a neighbor. Then the leader tells them the answer. Whoever was closest is the winner!

Solution: If you didn't sleep or take any breaks, the counting would take about thirty-two years.

Thingy

Props: Small slips of paper prepared in advance, as described below; a small basket in which to put them

Preparation: On small slips of paper, write the names of things like "snowman," "cough syrup," and "rubber ducky"

How to Play: Divide the class into small groups. Fold up the slips of paper and put them in a small basket. One child in each group draws a slip of paper, unfolds it, reads it silently, and then tries to describe the object to the other players on her team without saying the object's name. For the word "snowman," for example, the child could say, "There's snow outside. All the kids run outside to build a big figure in the snow." Whoever comes up with the solution first gets to draw the second slip of paper and describe the next word.

If a player accidentally says the word while trying to describe it, he is out, and names another player to continue.

Riddles

How to Play: Ask the children to answer these riddles:

What has a bridge, but you can't walk across it? (It also runs, but you can't catch it.)

Answer: A nose

What do you call a fly without wings?

Answer: A walk

What has six legs and two heads?

Answer: A horse and rider

What is so fragile that you can break it just by saying its name?

Answer: Silence

Why do black sheep eat less grass than white sheep?

Answer: Because there aren't as many black sheep.

You can make a regular riddle break or time in the week, and ask children to create teams that quiz or compete with each other.

Time Guesses

Props: Paper; pens or pencils; a stopwatch

How to Play: This game helps children estimate short lengths of time. Ask them a question such as, "How long will it take for us to sing 'Twinkle, Twinkle, Little Star'?" The children write down their guesses.

    Then they perform the action as a group, in this case singing the song, and one child times them with a stopwatch. Whoever had the closest guess gets a point.

Twinkle, twinkle

Continue with other questions:

- How long will it take for us to sing "Happy Birthday"?
- ...for Frank to find the page about worms in the animal dictionary?
- ...for Tina to go outside and pick three blades of grass as quickly as she can?
- ...to do three math problems?
- ...for everyone to draw a donkey?
- ...for the leader to hand out pieces of paper to everyone in the group?

Crossword Puzzle

Props: Short stories or articles for every child; a blackboard; chalk

How to Play: The children all have copies of a story or short article in front of them. One child chooses a long word from the text and writes it vertically on the board in capital letters, from top to bottom. Based on an order determined by seat assignment or called out by the leader, the other children come up one by one and add other words from the text, like a crossword puzzle: across or down. They must use at least one letter that is already on the board. You could also play this without a starting text.

The game is over after a predetermined period of time has elapsed or when the leader decides the players are starting to run out of space on the board.

Example:

```
        H
        A
    G R A I N
        V
  W H E A T
        S
        T
```

small groups

Work Clothes

Props: Paper; pens or pencils

How to Play: Divide the class into small groups. Players try to come up with jobs that require a uniform or certain clothing. Whoever lists the most jobs within two minutes is the winner in their group.

Examples

- police officer
- firefighter
- mail carrier
- soldier
- pilot
- waiter/waitress
- judge
- lawyer
- cook
- nurse
- doctor
- forest ranger

89

Clock-Face Puzzle

Props: A blackboard; chalk

How to Play: Draw a clock face on the board and mark the numbers from 1 to 12. Working individually, the children then need to figure out where to draw a straight line dividing the clock in half so that the numbers in each half add up to 39.

Answer: The line starts between 9 and 10, and ends between 3 and 4.

Endless Jokes

How to Play: One child tells his favorite joke but leaves off the punch line. The quick thinker who comes up with the correct punch line, or at least a good one, gets to tell her joke next.

any size

91

Number Miracle

Props: A blackboard; chalk

How to Play: On a blackboard, a three-by-three grid is filled in with any nine consecutive numbers. The following is the easiest version:

    1   2   3
    4   5   6
    7   8   9

The player chooses any three numbers in the grid, one at a time, but each cannot be in the same row or column as the others. The leader claims to know ahead of time what the total of the three numbers will be; it will always be the sum of the three numbers in the diagonals. In this case:

$1 + 5 + 9 = 15$. The other diagonal, $3 + 5 + 7$, also equals 15.

For example, let's say the player chooses 2 as the first number. The game leader circles the 2, and crosses out all the numbers in the same row (1, 3) and column (5, 8).

Then the player chooses a second number, maybe the 9. The leader circles the number 9, and again crosses out all the numbers in the same row and column. Now there is only one number left for the player to choose: 4.

Altogether, the player has chosen 2, 9, and 4. When they are added up, the total is 15, as predicted.

Variation: The game is more exciting when the grid is filled with higher numbers, or has more squares. In a four-by-four grid, the player gets to choose four numbers; in a five-by-five grid, five numbers; etc.

Example: In the four-by-four grid, the numbers in the diagonals add up to 34. No matter which four numbers the player chooses, they will add up to 34.

Eighteen
in a Square

Props: A piece of paper with a six-by-six grid drawn on it for each child; pens or pencils

How to Play: Each child has a piece of paper with a six-by-six grid on it. The assignment is to plant eighteen "trees" in such a way that each row, across and down, has three trees in it.

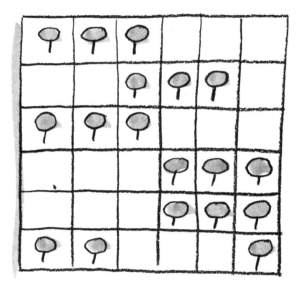

Once players think they have found the solution, they can switch papers with a neighbor to check their answers and be amazed by how many different solutions there are.

Letter Hide-and-Seek

Props: Paper; pens or pencils

How to Play: The children are given a certain combination of letters, and they have five three minutes to list as many words as possible containing those letters in order; for instance, "a-r-n" (e.g., yarn, barnyard, carnation).

Once the time is up, the results are scored as follows: If letters were added only at the beginning or at the end of the letter group, the word gets one point (e.g., barn, warn, Arnold). If letters were added at both ends, the word gets two points (e.g., carnival, earnest).

Novelties

Props: Paper; pens or pencils

How to Play: Each player has exactly five minutes to write down as many things as possible that were discovered or invented during the last two hundred years (e.g., lightbulb, computer, plastic, automobiles, Jell-O, contact lenses).

Then everyone has another five minutes to think up inventions or discoveries for the next two hundred years.

All the ideas are read aloud. The winner is the person who comes up with the most ideas.

95

Missing Consonants

Props: A blackboard; chalk

How to Play: One child thinks up a short sentence and instead of writing the full words writes only the vowels in the words on the board. "Today the sun is shining," for example, becomes "oay e u i ii."

The others try to come up with their own sentences using this vowel pattern. Whoever is the first to come up with a sentence that fits is the winner and gets to write the vowels for a new sentence on the board.

Variation: For a game of "missing vowels," follow the same rules, but write only the consonants from the sentence on the board. Using the above example, the player would write "td th sn s shnng."

The Vowel-Consonant Game

How to Play: In five minutes, who can come up with the most words that fit this vowel-consonant pattern: CVCCVC?

Possible solutions: winner, hammer, garden, gander, ladles, singer.

Dice Bingo

Props: Each pair of players will require a set of dice; two different colors of marker; a piece of paper with a grid containing numbers on it, as described below

Preparation: Draw a six-by-six grid on a piece of paper and insert the numbers 1 to 36 in the boxes in any order. Make as many photocopies of this numbered grid as you will need so that each pair of players will have their own copy.

How to Play: The leader divides the group into pairs and chooses one player in each pair to start. Make sure each player has a different-colored marker. The first player begins by rolling two—or even three—dice at once. She may either add, subtract, multiply, or divide the numbers that have been rolled, and then crosses out the answer in the grid. Then it's her opponent's turn. The winner is the first person to cross out four adjoining squares horizontally, vertically, or diagonally.

Example: A child rolls a 5 and a 6. He may cross out either the 1 (6 – 5), the 11 (6 + 5), or the 30 (6 × 5).

Reading Lips

How to Play: One child is sent out of the room. The rest of the children think up a longish word for the lip-reader to guess, and they choose someone to say the word. For example, the word might be "cucumber," and Polly is chosen to say it. The other children think of other words.

Then the first child is called back into the room. He is told the secret word, in this case, "cucumber."

At the signal to start, all the children start "talking" at the same time. They say their words over and over, but without making a sound. The guesser looks carefully at their moving lips and tries to figure out who is saying the secret word.

To make this into a competitive game, someone can time each guesser, and the player with the fastest time wins.

Knocking and Clapping

How to Play: In this game, two-digit numbers are communicated by knocking and clapping. A ten is represented by one knock on the table or wall, and a one is represented by one clap. For example, the leader or one of the children is thinking of the number 53; she or he knocks five times and claps three times.

Now everyone has to pay close attention. The leader picks one player to start, and she can knock and clap in whatever order she wants. If she's thinking of the number 84, for example, she could knock three times, clap twice, knock four times, clap twice, and finally knock once more. Who can guess the number? It's not easy, but it's fun, and the person who guesses correctly first gets to knock and clap the number of their choosing in the next round.

whole group

Ghost Journey

How to Play: The lead player thinks of a famous person or character, one whom everyone will know (Harry Potter, Spider-Man, president of the United States, etc.). But, of course, he doesn't tell the group who the famous person is. Instead, he will spell out the name of the person in code. For consonants, he names geographical locations that start with the same letter as the consonant in the famous person's name. For vowels, he knocks on a tabletop or other hard surface: one knock for "a," two knocks for "e," and so on.

To start, he tells the other players that a ghost is going to lead them on a journey.

Example: The famous character is Spider-Man.

Lead player: "The first stop on our journey is Seattle (or Spain, South Carolina, etc.).

"The next stop on our journey is Paris (or Pennsylvania, Portugal, etc.).

"Now the ghost will speak to us. [Knocks three times to indicate the letter 'i.']

"The next stop on our journey is Dallas (or Denver, Denmark, etc.).

"Now the ghost will speak to us again. [Knocks twice for the letter 'e.']"

The lead player continues like this until someone guesses Spider-Man. The first player who guesses correctly comes up with the next famous person and delivers the clues.

Mystery Letter

How to Play: One child leaves the room while the others decide on a secret letter; for example, N. Then the guesser is called back into the room. He is allowed to ask the others up to ten questions. Each question is answered by three children who are called on by the leader after they raise their hands to indicate they have thought of a response containing the mystery letter. It doesn't matter whether the answers are true, false, or nonsensical.

Example: The guesser might ask, "Which animal lays eggs?" Someone answers, "a hen," while another says, "a rhino," and a third person chooses "elephant."

The guesser tries to use these answers to draw conclusions about the mystery letter.

Next, he might ask, "What color is a lemon?" The responses are "green" or "brown," maybe even "inky blue"; however, "yellow" won't be one of the answers, since it doesn't contain the mystery letter. The guesser continues to ask questions until he figures out the mystery letter and says it out loud. Once he guesses correctly, he gets to pick the next player to leave the room.

The Riddles

1. The Pants-Pocket Problem

Mr. Snicklefritz notices that his pants pocket is empty, but there's still something in it. What could it be?

Answer: A hole

2. Day by Day

Which letters can be found in every day of the week?

Answer: D, A, Y

3. Animal Riddle

What animal is hiding in these letters? (Tip: Instead of saying the letters aloud, perhaps write them on a blackboard.)

   L P H N

Answer: Elephant

4. Guessing Game

What's left when you take the ant out of the plantain?

Answer: The plain

5. Apartment-House Mouse

Paula, the apartment-house mouse, is trying to get in shape. She wants to do this by climbing stairs. She starts on the fourth floor, climbs up five stories, down seven, up six, down three, and up four again. What floor is she on now?

Answer: 4 + 5 – 7 + 6 – 3 + 4 = 9; Paula is on the ninth floor.

6. 5 5 5 5 5

Add a symbol somewhere in this row of fives to make an equation equaling 500.
Answer: 555 – 55 = 500

7. Directions

Paul took a wonderful picture of the sunset. In which direction was he pointing the camera?
Answer: West

8. Vacation Driving

The Snicklefritz family is driving south for their summer vacation. The Breadcrumb family is driving in the opposite direction. Which direction is that?
Answer: The Breadcrumbs are driving north.

9. From 1 to 10

Add up all the numbers from 1 to 10. What's the total?
Answer: 55

10. Alphabetical Months

If you organize all the months alphabetically, which one comes first and which one is last?
Answer: The first month would be April, and the last one would be September.

11. New Order

If we list the days of the week in alphabetical order, which day would be first and which would be last?

Answer: Friday would be first, and Wednesday would be last.

12. Welcome to the Club!

Jeremy and his friends have started a strange club. Only children whose first names have three or more syllables can join their club. Write down the names of all the people in your group who could join the club.

13. Polar Bear Birthday

Pierre the polar bear has lots of friends. This was apparent on his birthday. Each guest brought him 5 fish. Even though Pauly Penguin stole 2 of the fish, there are still 198 fish left in Pierre's gift pile. How many friends came to Pierre's birthday party?

Answer: 40

14. The Carrot Quirk

Reginald Rabbit eats one carrot every Sunday. On Mondays he eats two carrots, on Tuesdays four carrots, and so on.

1. On which day of the week does Reginald eat sixteen carrots?
2. How many carrots does he eat on Saturdays?
3. How many carrots total does he eat every week?

Answers: Thursday; 64; 127

15. Beary Hungry

If five polar bears can eat five fish in three minutes, how much time will eighteen polar bears need to eat eighteen fish?

Answer: Three minutes

16. Weekday Riddle

Tomorrow I will say, "The day before yesterday was Saturday."
   What day is it today?
   If the day after tomorrow is Thursday, what day was it the day before yesterday?
   If July 28th is a Friday, what will the date be on the following Tuesday?

Answers: Sunday; Sunday; August 1

17. In the Hospital

Robbie Rabbit was hopping too fast, and he broke his leg. He was admitted to the hospital on Monday, November 1st. Robbie got to go home on November 30th. What day of the week was it?

Answer: Tuesday

18. Ice-Cream Scoops

Mr. and Mrs. Snicklefritz are sitting in the ice cream parlor. Mrs. Snicklefritz looks at her ice cream dish and at the one in front of her husband, and says, "If you give me one of your scoops of ice cream, I'll have twice as many as you." But Mr. Snicklefritz doesn't want to do that. He says, "Why don't you give me one of your scoops of ice cream, and then we'll have the same number." Can you solve the puzzle and figure out how many scoops of ice cream are in each dish?

Answer: Mrs. Snicklefritz has seven scoops, and her husband has five.

19. In the Ice Cream Parlor

Rusty orders six dishes of ice cream with three scoops each. Paula wants just as many scoops, but in two dishes. How many scoops are in each of her dishes?

Answer: Nine scoops in each

20. Boomerang

Lisa says, "I bet I can throw a ball in such a way so that it flies away from me, suddenly changes direction, and then comes back to me all by itself."

Is that possible?

Answer: Yes, if Lisa throws the ball straight up in the air.

21. Riddle Bears

In a bag of gummy bears, there are exactly three red bears, three green ones, three yellow ones, and three white ones left. How many gummy bears would you have to take out of the bag in order to make sure you had at least three of the same color?

Answer: Nine

22. Cookie Problem

In a cookie jar, there are ten butter cookies and ten chocolate-chip cookies. Tom sneaks over to the cookie jar in the middle of the night and tries to figure out:

- How many cookies do I need to take out of the jar if I want to make sure to get at least two of each kind?
- How many cookies do I need to take out of the jar if I want to make sure to get at least two butter cookies?

Answer: Twelve cookies; twelve cookies

23. Uncles, Aunts, and Other Relatives

Emma is Willy's niece, but she's not Ginny's niece, even though Ginny is Willy's sister and Willy isn't married. How can that be? And how is Emma related to Ginny?

Answer: Emma is Ginny's daughter.

24. In Pairs

Name some things that only come in pairs, or that can only be bought in pairs. After two minutes, read your answers aloud. Whoever comes up with the most is the winner.

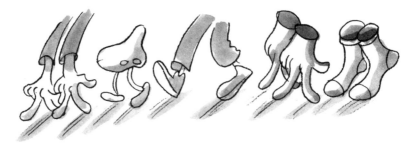

Answers: Eyes, nostrils, hands, arms, legs, feet, gloves, earrings, shoes, socks, slippers.

25. Time Problem

Three clocks show three different times. One clock is a little bit fast, one is a little bit slow, and one of them shows the right time. The clocks say 10:05, 9:56, and 10:11. Which clock is correct?

Answer: The first one—it's 10:05.

26. Sixty-Five Cents

What's the smallest number of coins you can use to make up exactly sixty-five cents?

Answer: Four coins—two quarters, a dime, and a nickel

27. Snail-Shell Settlement

Elvira Slime lives on a street with ten snail-shell houses. The houses are numbered 1 to 10. If Elvira adds up all the house numbers that are lower than hers,

the total is three times her own house number. What number is on Elvira's house?

Answer: Elvira Slime lives in house number 7. All the smaller house numbers add up to 21 (1 + 2 + 3 + 4 + 5 + 6), which is three times as large as 7.

28. At the Movies

The movie *Shipwrecked in an Inner Tube* is sold out. The first people start showing up an hour before show time. Then the number of audience members doubles every ten minutes. After sixty minutes, the movie theater is full. When was it half full?

Answer: Ten minutes before the movie started.

29. In-Between Numbers

- Which multiples of four are found between 10 and 19?
- Which uneven numbers are between 10 and 16?
- What's the biggest three-digit number that you can make with the digits 3, 5, and 7?

Answers: 12, 16; 11, 13, 15; 753

30. Birthday on Mars

A year on Mars lasts twice as long as a year on Earth, so how old would you be if you lived on Mars? How old would your parents be? Your teacher? Your grandma?

How old would a thirty-six-year-old Martian be on Earth?

Answer: If you are eight years old, then you would be four on Mars. A thirty-six-year-old Martian would be seventy-two in Earth years.

31. Seven Dwarfs

Once upon a time there were seven dwarfs who were all brothers. They were all born two years apart. The youngest dwarf is seven years old. How old is his oldest brother?

Answer: Nineteen

32. A Dog and His Master

Right now, Mr. Potts is exactly five times as old as his dog Fluffy.

In five years, Mr. Potts will only be three times as old as Fluffy.

If Fluffy is five years old now, how old will Mr. Potts be in five years?

Note: If you want to make the assignment harder, don't tell the children how old Fluffy is now!

Answer: In five years, Mr. Potts will be thirty years old.

33. Month by Month

Imagine that each month had the same number of days: thirty. Would a year then be longer or shorter?

Answer: Shorter (12 × 30 = 360)

34. Arithmetic Acrobatics

Which two numbers have the same result whether you multiply them or add them together?

Answer: 2 × 2 = 4; 2 + 2 = 4

35. Salad Days

Elvira Slime and her friend Adelaide have found a head of lettuce with twenty leaves. Because Elvira found the lettuce first, she gets one more leaf than her friend does. How many lettuce leaves does Elvira get, and how many does Adelaide get?

Answer: Elvira gets ten and a half leaves, and Adelaide gets nine and a half.

36. Counting Ears

If you were to count all the ears in your city and divide the result by two, what number would you have?

Answer: The number of all the living creatures in the city

37. Penguin Head Count

Pierre the polar bear visits a penguin class and asks the teacher, "How many students are in your class?"

"Oh," says the teacher, "I don't know exactly. I can only tell you that there are fewer than thirty, but more than twenty. The children can make groups of two, three, four, six, and eight without anyone left over." "Aha," says Pierre, and thinks long and hard.

Can you figure out how many students are in the penguin class?

Answer: The class has twenty-four students.

38. Distance

Carla leaves San Jose at eight in the morning and starts driving toward San Francisco. Carla's average speed is 35 mph. At the same time, her friend Harriet leaves San Francisco and starts driving toward San Jose, averaging 50 mph.

At the moment when they meet, which one will be farther away from San Francisco?

Answer: Since the two ladies will be at the same point when they meet, they will be the same distance from San Francisco.

39. Extraterrestrial Money Problems

Imagine this: On Pluto, instead of dollars and cents, there is a currency made up of plups, plips, and plaps. When you do the conversion, you realize that there are five plups in a plap, and one plip is equal to two plaps. Which unit of currency is worth the most: a plup, a plap, or a plip?

Answer: one plip = two plaps = ten plups

40. Extraterrestrial Time Problems

If a day on Planet Androx lasts as long as two weeks on Earth, how long would an hour be on Androx, measured in Earth time?

Answer: Fourteen times as long, so fourteen Earth hours

41. Addendum

Which word can you add on to the words in each list to make common terms?

- pine, money, family
- salt, mineral, rain
- head, stomach, tooth
- basket, snow, disco
- bird, doll, glass

Answers: tree; water; ache; ball; house

42. Mother and Daughter

Jenny is fourteen years old, and her mother is thirty-eight. How many years ago was her mother exactly three times as old as Jenny?

Answer: Two years ago. Jenny was twelve then, and her mother was thirty-six.

43. Baker's Math

A crate filled with flour weighs 15 pounds. The baker takes out half of the flour, and notices that the box with the rest of the flour still weighs 9 pounds. Who can be the first to figure out how heavy the empty crate is?

Answer: The crate weighs 3 pounds. 15 lbs. – 9 lbs. = 6 lbs. (the weight of half the flour); 6 lbs. × 2 = 12 lbs. (the total weight of the flour); 15 lbs. – 12 lbs. = 3 lbs.

44. Flag Lesson

1. How many stripes are on the U.S. flag?
2. What do the stripes stand for?
3. What do the stars on the U.S. flag stand for?
4. What do the colors red, white, and blue symbolize on the U.S. flag?

Answers: 1. Thirteen; 2. The thirteen original colonies; 3. The stars stand for the individual states; 4. Red = bravery; white = purity; blue = justice.

45. Secret Language

Who can decipher the secret language first?

Tha twasn treal lys oh ardaf terall.

It looks hard, but you can read it in one glance. If you want to make it a little bit harder, write the sentence backward in addition to moving the spaces around. The result then looks like this:

.th girll are drah tib elt tila stahT

You can encode all kinds of secret messages using this pattern.

46. Musical Quick Thinkers

Who can be the first child to come up with a song that has the word "sea" in its lyrics?

Other key words you might use: sun, sky, day, hill, ocean, May, woods, birds, snow, night.

Possible solutions:
- *"My Bonnie Lies over the Ocean" (My Bonnie lies over the ocean, my Bonnie lies over the sea . . .)*
- *"Puff the Magic Dragon" (Puff, the magic dragon, lived by the sea . . .)*
- *"Under the Sea"*
- *"America, the Beautiful" (. . . and crown thy good with brotherhood, from sea to shining sea")*

47. How Time Flies

Mrs. Fisher says to her neighbor, "My son is turning sixteen today. On his next birthday, he'll be twenty." Has Mrs. Fisher forgotten how to count, or could she be right? What do you think?

Answer: Mrs. Fisher's son was born on February 29th, so he only has a birthday every four years.

48. Mischief-Maker

Which object does not belong with the rest in each list?

1. trumpet, flute, violin, harmonica, tuba

2. dog, goose, cat, sheep, cow

3. pliers, hammer, screwdriver, fork, drill

4. toaster, hair dryer, scissors, iron, mixer

5. tomato, strawberry, radish, cucumber, cherry

Answers: 1. violin; 2. goose; 3. fork; 4. scissors; 5. cucumber (not red) or radish (not a fruit)

49. Dice Math I

As we know, the number of dots on opposite sides of a die always add up to 7. For example, if someone rolls a 2, we know that the bottom side of the die is a 5.

Kevin rolls three dice at once. If he adds all three together, he gets 8. What would be the total of the numbers on the bottom of the dice?

Answer: Thirteen, because 21 − 8 = 13

50. Dice Math II

Once you think about it a little bit, this dice game shouldn't be too hard, either. The game leader builds a little tower by stacking three dice on the table. If the topmost die has three dots showing on top, what is the sum of the five (top and bottom) faces of the dice you can't see?

Answer: Since the sum of two opposite die faces is always 7, the sum of 3 dice would be 21. The (visible) number on top of the dice tower (in our example, 3) is subtracted from 21, which gives us the sum of the remaining (hidden) surfaces: 18.

51. Dice Odds

Think carefully: If you were to roll a die only once, which of the following would be least likely?

1. You roll an odd number.

2. You roll a number larger than three.

3. You roll a number smaller than three.

Answer: 3. You roll a number smaller than three.

52. Tennis Tournament

There are sixteen contestants in a round-robin tennis tournament.

How many games have to take place before the winner is determined?

Answer: Fifteen games

53. Geese and Goats

Farmer Wolf has geese and goats. Today he counted the legs on his beloved animals and realized that there are exactly thirty-six of them. Can you figure out how many geese and how many goats the farmer has? How many possible answers are there?

Answer: Seven possible answers (geese–goats: 2–8, 4–7, 6–6, 8–5, 10–4, 12–3, 14–2)

54. Letter Puzzle

The following letters are written on the board: JFMAMJJASOND.
    What could they mean?

Answer: They are the first letters of all the months.

55. Snail Race

Four snails—Toby, Pete, Lori, and Elvira—are competing in the annual snail race, with the following results: Lori finished four hours ahead of Elvira. Pete crawled across the finish line eight hours before Toby. Toby needed six hours longer to finish the course than Lori did.

In what order did the snails cross the finish line?

Answer: Pete, Lori, Elvira, Toby

56. Mother's Day

Mother's Day is always the second Sunday in May. What is the earliest possible date for this holiday, and what's the latest possible date?

Answer: The earliest date would be May 8th, and the latest would be May 14th.

57. Mirror Letters

Which eleven capital letters look the same when you read them in a mirror?

Answer: A, H, I, M, O, T, U, V, W, X, Y

58. Birth Year

Imagine you were born in an odd-numbered year (like 1995). Will you celebrate your 50th birthday in an odd or an even year?

Answer: In an odd year. Your 1st birthday is in an even year, your 2nd in an odd year, your 3rd in an even one, etc.

59. The Brilliant Sister

Peter says to his sister Bitsy, "Because I'm twice as old as you, I'm twice as smart, too." His sister responds, "Yes, but in five years I'll be twice as old as I am now, and you won't." Peter is dumbfounded, and he stops to calculate how old he and his sister will be in five years. Do you know the answer?

Answer: Bitsy will be ten years old in five years, and Peter will be fifteen.

60. Heavyweight

Together, Tom and his father weigh 280 pounds. Tom's father weighs three times as much as Tom does. How much does Tom weigh?

Answer: Tom weighs 70 pounds.

61. Logical Letter Lists

Continue each series by adding the appropriate group of letters:

1. ABC DEF GHI JKL...
2. AZ BY CX DW...
3. ABD BCE CDF DEG...
4. ZYX WVU TSR QPO...

Answers: 1. MNO; 2. EV; 3. EFH; 4. NML

62. Think about It!

Which two numbers make a one-digit number when you multiply them, but a two-digit number when you add them?

Answer: 1 and 9; 1 × 9 = 9 (one digit); 1 + 9 = 10 (two digits)

63. Bus Route

A city bus leaves the bus yard with no passengers in it. At the first bus stop, two people get on, and at the next stop, five more. At the one after that, seven people get on and three get off. At the next stop, five people get on and six get off. At the stop after that, three people get on and one gets off.

Question: How many stops has the bus made so far?

Answer: Five

64. Two Digits

Think carefully: How many two-digit numbers are there?

Answer: There are ninety two-digit numbers.

65. Around the Sun

1. How many planets orbit the sun?
2. Which planet is closer to the sun: the Earth or Mars?
3. What are the names of the planets?
4. Which planet is closest to the sun?

Answers: 1. Eight; 2. Earth; 3. Mercury, Venus, Earth, Mars, Jupiter, Saturn, Uranus, Neptune; 4. Mercury

Alphabetical List of Games

Games with Special Requirements

Games Requiring Props

Games in Which Physical Contact Might Be Involved

Games Requiring a Large Space

Games Requiring Going Outdoors